When Rosa Parks Martin Luther King, Junior

Written by Zoë Clarke

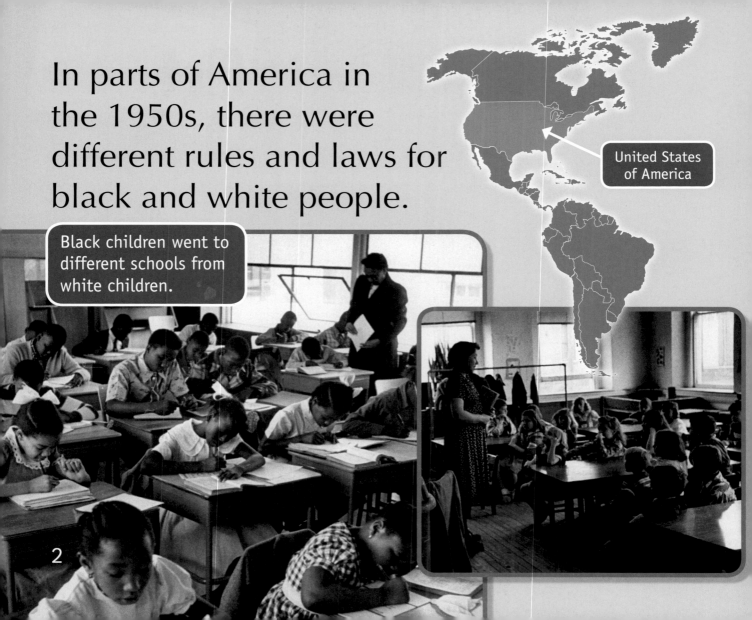

In parts of America in the 1950s, there were different rules and laws for black and white people.

Black children went to different schools from white children.

United States of America

2

On buses, black and white people couldn't sit together.

4

If the bus was full,
white people sat.
Black people had to stand.

Rosa Parks was a black woman who didn't agree with this rule.

In 1955, she didn't give up her seat to a white man, so the police took her away.

Rosa Parks at the police station

Martin Luther King, Junior agreed with Rosa Parks, and asked black people not to use buses.

Martin Luther King, Junior making a speech

black people walking to work instead of using the buses

9

Over 40,000 black people didn't use buses for 381 days until the rule was changed to let black and white people sit together.

Rosa Parks sitting at the front of the bus

Martin Luther King, Junior sitting next to a white man on the bus

11

Martin Luther King, Junior on a march to try to change laws for black people

Rosa Parks and Martin Luther King, Junior helped to change other rules and laws so that everyone was treated the same.

12

Rosa Parks getting a medal

Martin Luther King, Junior receiving the Nobel Peace Prize

13

Fighting for change

Black people and white people are not treated the same.

Martin Luther King, Junior asks black people not to use the buses.

Rosa Parks is taken away by the police for not giving up her seat.

The rules are changed. Black people and white people can sit together on the buses.

40,000 black people walk to work.

Rosa Parks and Martin Luther King, Junior carry on with their work.

15

Ideas for reading

Written by Gillian Howell
Primary Literacy Consultant

Learning objectives: (reading objectives correspond with Yellow band; all other objectives correspond with Diamond band) use phonics to read unknown or difficult words; understand underlying themes, causes and points of view; understand how writers use different structures to create coherence; use the techniques of dialogic talk to explore ideas, topics or issues; improvise using a range of drama strategies and conventions to explore themes such as hopes, fears, desires; select words and language drawing on their knowledge of literary features and formal and informal writing

Curriculum links: Citizenship: Living in a diverse world; History: What can we learn about recent history by studying the life of a famous person?

High frequency words: did, not, that, black, people, white, should, be, how, were, way, if, got, had, who, her, took, many, with, one, them, over, so

Interest words: America, people, police, different, water fountains, wrong, Nobel Peace Prize

Resources: paper, pens, pencils, ICT

Word count: 201

Getting started

- Read the title together and ask the children if they know who Rosa Parks and Martin Luther King, Junior were. Talk for a few moments about the civil rights movement in America and how different races were or are sometimes treated differently. Ask the children if they have any experience of this.

- Turn to the back cover and read the blurb together. Ask the children to say what they think the phrase "fought for change" means. What sort of events do they think will be in the book?

- Discuss the different non-fiction features the children expect to find as they read, e.g. captioned photos, and why.

Reading and responding

- Look together at the illustrations on pp2–3 to orientate the children. Read the opening sentence together. Ask them to discuss it with a partner and suggest from the photos ways in which black and white people were treated differently and give a personal response.